CW00351672

Say It With Flowers

By **Meic Povey** and **Johnny Tudor**

This play was produced by Sherman Cymru and first performed at the Sherman Theatre, Cardiff on Wednesday 15 May 2013.

Meic Povey and Johnny Tudor assert their moral right to be identified as the authors of this work.

Cover image: Kirsten McTernan
Design: Rhys Huws
Typeset in Wales by Eira Fenn Gaunt
Printed in Wales by Cambrian Printers, Aberystwyth.

CAST

Emily	Heledd Gwynn
Maisie	Lynn Hunter
Young Dot	Gillian Kirkpatrick
Old Dot	Ruth Madoc
Roger	Matt Nalton
Freddie	Aled Pedrick
Pianist	Dyfan Jones/Greg Palmer

PRODUCTION TEAM

Director: Pia Furtado
Designer: Georgia Lowe
Lighting Designer: Katharine Williams
Composer/Musical Director: Dyfan Jones
Sound Designer: Mike Beer
Assistant Director: Julia Thomas
Casting: Camilla Evans/Kate Perridge
Stage Manager: Brenda Knight
Deputy Stage Manager: Natasha Nicholls
Assistant Stage Manager: Charlotte Neville
Wardrobe Assistant: Angharad Griffin
Assistant Stage Manager (Apprentice): Joanna Jones

THANKS

Emily Squires
Amy Hodge
Rhian Morris
Peter, Joe and Tom Knight
Alliance Carpet Mills Ltd., Dinas Enterprise Centre, Porth
Ulster Carpet Mills Ltd.
Laura Martin, Scenery Hire Ltd.
Print Centre Cardiff
Mappa Mundi Theatre Company

SHERMAN
CYMRU

We aim to make and present great theatre that is ambitious, inventive and memorable for our audiences, and to create strong, responsive and enriching relationships with our communities. We produce work in both English and Welsh, and tour widely within Wales and the UK.
For more information about Sherman Cymru events visit -
www.shermancymru.co.uk

40 Appeal

Following on from the excitement of 2012 with the reopening of the Sherman building, 2013 has a celebration of its own as we mark the 40th anniversary of the original opening of the Sherman Theatre.

In recognition of Sherman's anniversary year we are introducing a new opportunity for you to support the work of the company whilst receiving some great benefits.

For 2013 only, in return for a donation of £40 (single), £73 (couple) or £19.73 (Under 25s) you will receive the following benefits:
• Advance notice of the season's performances and activities
• Seasonal priority booking
• Your name on the Sherman Cymru website
• 10% discount on post-show drinks at the bar
• Name on the 40 donations wall in the foyer
• Discounted tickets to selected performances in the 40th anniversary season
• Invitation to an exclusive 40th birthday party in the autumn
• Backstage tour with a member of Sherman Cymru staff

By supporting Sherman Cymru you will be doing your bit to help secure the arts in Wales for this year, next year and the next 40 years!

To join and for further information please contact Emma Goad, Head of Development on 029 2064 6975 or visit www.shermancymru.co.uk/40-appeal.

v

Heledd Gwynn
Emily

Having been a member of the National Youth Theatre of Wales for three years, Heledd decided to study acting and became a student at the Royal Welsh College of Music and Drama. She will be graduating this summer.

Theatre
A Provincial Life (National Theatre Wales); *A Month in the Country, Hamlet, The Children's Hour, Beasts and Beauties* (The Richard Burton Company).

At the end of her second year she won a Laurence Olivier Bursary Award.

Theatre

*The Snow Queen, Six (*Sherman Cymru*); Sound is to Speech as Speech is to Sound, A Kiss on the Bottom* (Sherman Theatre); *The Grapes of Wrath, The Druid's Rest, Night Must Fall, Brassed Off, Y Mabinogi, The Ballad of Megan Morgan, Oh! What a Lovely War, Romeo and Juliet* (Clwyd Theatr Cymru); *Roots and Wings* (Frank Vickery Productions); *Shadow of a Boy* (National Theatre).

Television

Stella (Sky 1); *Baker Boys, The Legend of Dick & Dom, The Commander, Casualty, High Hopes, Belonging, The Story of Tracy Beaker, Outside the Rules, Tales from Pleasure Beach, Care, Food for Ravens, Civvies, Morphine & Dolly Mixtures, Streetlife* (BBC Wales); *Mine All Mine, Flint Street Nativity* (ITV); *Family Affairs* (Channel 5).

Film

Submarine (Film Four); *Patagonia* (Rainy Day Films, Boom Films, Boomerang); *Death of a Double Act, Arthur's Dyke* (Quirky Films); *Very Annie Mary* (Canal+, Film Four, Dragon Pictures); *House (*House Productions); *Restoration* (Miramax Films).

Radio

Spoils of Victory, Station Road, 4 Short Stories, A Child's Christmas in Wales, The Mark of Zorro, Skeletons (BBC Radio).

Lynn Hunter
Maisie

Gillian Kirkpatrick
Young Dot

Gillian trained at the Royal Conservatoire of Scotland, Glasgow and the Royal Academy of Music.

Theatre
Chess (Union Theatre); *Sweeney Todd* (Adelphi Theatre & Chichester Festival Theatre); *Hairspray* (Original UK Tour); *Billy Elliot* (Victoria Palace Theatre); *Into The Woods* (Royal Opera House); *Blood Brothers* (Phoenix Theatre & UK Tour); *Carmen* (New Vic Theatre Stoke and Tour); *Sweeney Todd, Paradise Moscow* (Opera North); *Charlotte: Life or Theatre?* (Drill Hall); *A Tale of Two Cities* (Birmingham Alexandra Theatre); *I Love You, You're Perfect, Now Change* (Comedy Theatre); *The Rink* (Orange Tree Theatre, Richmond); *Company* (Manchester Library Theatre); *Me & My Girl, My Cousin Rachel* (Perth Rep Theatre); *Macbeth* (German Tour).

Television and Film
Bottle Neck (Urban Myth Productions); *Revisited* (Bournemouth University).

Further Credits
Billy Elliot (original cast recording); *Sweeney Todd* (Adelphi Theatre cast recording).
Workshops include *The Last Ship* - a new musical written by Sting (Live Theatre, Newcastle); *Rehab* (The Arts Theatre).

Ruth is a graduate of the Royal Academy of Dramatic Art and is best known for her portrayal of Gladys Pugh in the classic comedy series *Hi-De-Hi!* for which she was nominated for a BAFTA.

Ruth Madoc
Old Dot

Theatre
Twelfth Night (Regents Park Theatre London); *Calendar Girls* (David Pugh); *Hi-De-Hi!, Mixed Feelings, Give Us a Crew, Find the Lady, A Taste of Honey, Dark Stranger, Don't Start Without Me, A Murder is Announced, Verdict, Niteclub Confidential, Bless the Bride, Gypsy, Phantom of the Opera, 42nd Street, Annie; Under Milk Wood.*

Television
Morecombe and Wise, Bob Monkhouse, Hunter's Walk, Lloyd George, Blankety Blank, Big Top (BBC); *Give Us a Clue, Cluedo, An Actor's Life for Me, Animal Ark, The Famous Five, Jack of Hearts, Mine All Mine* (ITV); *Blackpool to Benidorm* (Sky). She also appeared as the infamous Dafydd's mother in the BAFTA award winning comedy *Little Britain.*

Film
Fiddler on the Roof (Cartier Productions); *The Prince and the Pauper, Very Annie Mary* (Canal+, Film Four, Dragon Productions); *Under Milk Wood* (Timon Productions).

Matt Nalton
Roger

Matt trained at the Royal Central School of Speech and Drama on the BA Acting course. Theatre whilst training includes *Guys and Dolls*, *A Midsummer Night's Dream*, *Emperor of The Moon* and *Merrily We Roll Along*.

Theatre
Black Snow (Moscow Arts Theatre); *The Firework Makers Daughter* (Theatre By The Lake); *Matt Lucas and Friends* (Vaudeville Theatre); *Sleeping Beauty* (Castle Theatre); *Fiddler on the Roof* (Bridewell Theatre); *Whistle Down The Wind* (Greenwich Theatre); *Sweeney Todd* (Village Underground and Rose Theatre, Kingston).

Matt also performed for Her Majesty The Queen at Buckingham Palace in *A Celebration of Young People In The Performing Arts*. Matt was a BBC Performing Arts Bursary winner. He is also an accomplished Pianist, Musical Director and Published Composer.

Aled Pedrick
Freddie

Aled's passion for theatre was sparked at a very young age through his participation in the National and Urdd Eisteddfod- the highlight of which was receiving the prestigious Bryn Terfel scholarship at the age of seventeen before being offered a place at the Guildhall School of Music and Drama.

Theatre
The Sanger, Ceisio'i Bywyd Hi (Sherman Cymru); *The Pride* (English Theatre Company); *Deffro'r Gwanwyn* (Theatr Genedlaethol Cymru); *The Nutcracker* (Theatre Royal, Bath).

Television and Film
Doctor Who (BBC); *Lewis* (ITV); *Aki Nabalu* (Astro, Malaysia); *Con Passionate, Gari Tryfan, Teulu* (S4C).

Aled was thrilled to make his directorial debut earlier this year with Invertigo Theatre Company's production of *Saer Doliau* at the Finborough Theatre.

Greg Palmer
Pianist

Greg has composed, arranged and directed music for over one hundred professional theatre productions throughout the UK. Most recently he was composer and musical director for the Manchester Library Theatre production of *Mother Courage* and musical director for the UK premiere of *Summer of '42* for the Liverpool Institute of Performing Arts.

Theatre
Horrible Christmas (Sherman Theatre); *Deffro'r Gwanwyn* (Theatr Gendlaethol Cymru); *Romeo and Juliet, A Comedy of Errors* (Shakespeare Festival, Stafford); *Sweeney Todd, Company, Sugar, A Funny Thing Happened on the Way to the Forum* (New Wolsey Theatre); *Guys and Dolls* (Clwyd Theatr Cymru, Salisbury Playhouse and New Wolsey Theatre); *Happy End* (Nottingham Playhouse); *Pinocchio* (Salisbury Playhouse); *A Child's Christmas in Wales* (Theatr na nÓg); *Animal Farm, As You Like It* (Clwyd Theatr Cymru); *The Beggar's Opera* (Bridewell Theatre); *Twelfth Night, Millennium Mysteries, Leader of the Pack* (Belgrade Theatre); *Macbeth, Tunstall Tanzi, Good Golly Miss Molly* (New Victoria Theatre); *Maria Marten* (Lincoln Theatre Royal); *Chicago, Bitter Sweet, Barnstormers* (Century Theatre); *Sweet Charity* (Handstand); *The Gambler* (London Bubble); *One Step Beyond* (Theatre Royal Stratford East).

Meic Povey
Writer

Meic Povey was born in Snowdonia in 1950. His professional career began at seventeen as a stage manager with Theatr Cymru, where he worked on plays in both languages. In 1974 he joined the drama department of BBC Wales as assistant script editor on the very first series of the long running soap opera, *Pobol y Cwm*.

In 1981/82 he created and wrote *Taff Acre* for HTV Wales, a 26-part soap opera broadcast on ITV.

Theatre
Y Pry, Yr Anifail, Terfyn, Chwara Plant, Indian Country, Life of Ryan...and Ronnie (Sgript Cymru); *Yn Debyg Iawn i Ti a Fi, Tyner Yw'r Lleuad Heno* (Theatr Genedlaethol Cymru); *Fel Anifail, Wyneb yn Wyneb, Bonansa!, Tair* (Dalier Sylw); *Diwedd y Byd, Yr Hen Blant* (Cwmni Theatr Gwynedd); *Gwaed Oer, Perthyn, Sylw* (Royal Welsh College of Music and Drama/ Sgript Cymru).

Television and Film
Meistres y Chwarae, Y Filltir Sgwar, Bob a'i Fam, Talcen Caled, Teulu, Y Weithred, Yr Ynys, Y Cadfridog, Camau Troellog, Aelwyd Gartrefol, Sul y Blodau, Deryn (S4C); *Glas y Dorlan, Nos Sadwrn Bach* (BBC); *A Mind To Kill* (Lluniau Lliw, 4L Productions); *Nel, Babylon Bypassed, Taff Acre, Richard Burton's A Christmas Story* (HTV Wales).

Radio
Don't Buy a Winter Coat, Fire of the Dragon, You Shouldn't Have Come, Like An Animal, Take Me To Hafod Owen (BBC Wales).

In 2010 he was awarded his third BAFTA Cymru Award for best scriptwriter. He is an honorary fellow of the Royal Welsh College of Music and Drama, and has been bestowed with an honorary MA for services to Welsh drama by the University of Wales. In 2008 he was made an honorary fellow at Bangor University, North Wales.

Johnny Tudor
Writer

Johnny has embraced all forms of the business in his rich and varied career, appearing in musical comedy, pantomime, drama, television, radio and film. More recently Johnny has concentrated on drama as well as directing and writing; he has directed three pantomimes and a musical for S4C and also written a sitcom for Windsor Davies, Ruth Madoc and himself called *Arrivederci Rhondda* for BBC Wales.

Theatre
Cindy (Fortune Theatre, West End); *A Funny Thing Happened on the Way to the Forum* (National Tour); *Give Me the Moonlight - The Frankie Vaughan Story* (National Tour); *Turn on the Taps* (National Tour).

Television
Gavin & Stacey, *The Singing Straits*, *Miss Wales* (BBC); *Stella* (Sky); *High Hopes, Belonging, Arriverderci Rhondda* (BBC Wales); *Pobl y Cwm* (S4C); *Opportunity Knocks* (Thames Television); *3.2.* (Yorkshire Television); *Perfect Pitch* (HTV).

Johnny is grateful for his life-long friendship with Dorothy Squires and to have appeared with her at her famous Palladium Concert in 1970, without which this story could never have been told.

Pia Furtado
Director

Pia trained at the King's Head Theatre, National Theatre Studio and Young Vic Theatre.

Theatre Credits include: *Dirty Great Love Story* (Soho Theatre/New York/Pleasance Edinburgh. Fringe First Award); *Cinders* (Nabokov/Latitude Festival); *Nicked* (HighTide Festival/Criterion Showcase); *Romania 21* (Teatrul Tineretului, Pomania); *Dream* (Royal Shakespeare Company); *Our Miss Gibbs* (Finborough Theatre); *Parade* (Southside, Edinburgh. UK premiere); GBS (King's Head); *All My Sons* (Bloomsbury Theatre). As Assistant Director: *Freshwater* (SITI/TWP, New York); *The Merchant of Venice, A Midsummer Night's Dream* (Royal Shakespeare Company); *Flight 5065, A Girl in a Car with a Man* (Royal Court).

Opera Credits include: *Werther* (Scottish Opera); *Susanna* (Iford Arts Festival); *Cautionary Tales* (Opera North); *Werther, L'Histoire de Babar, Le Chouette Enhrumée* (Les Azuriales); *Coffee Cantata* (Wellcome Trust/Early Opera); *Venus and Adonis* (Blow/La Nuova Musica/Spitalfields Festival). **Upcoming productions include:** *L'Elisir D'Amone* (Opera Holland Park); *Acis and Galatea* (Iford Arts Festival)

Georgia Lowe
Designer

Georgia trained on the Motley Theatre Design course and was a Linbury Prize Finalist 2011. She was Trainee Designer for the Royal Shakespeare Company 2011-2012.

Theatre Design includes:
Facts, Fog, Blue Surge, Follow (Finborough Theatre); *Shallow Slumber, Lift* (Soho Theatre); *Ignorance* (Hampstead); *Pericles, Song of Songs* (Royal Shakespeare Company); *Promise* (Arts Ed); *Susanna* (Iford Arts); *After the Rainfall* (Curious Directive); *The Dark Side of Love* (RSC/Lift/World Shakespeare Festival); *Yellow* (Tête à Tête Opera); *Drowning on Dry Land* (Jermyn Street Theatre); *Amphibians* (Bridewell Theatre); *Return to Silence* (Curious Directive/Pleasance Theatre); *Legacy Falls* (New Players Theatre); *Departure Lounge* (Waterloo East); *Whispering Happiness* (Tristan Bates Theatre); *I am Montana* (Arcola Studio).

She is currently designing *Acis and Galatea* for Iford Opera and *The Ruling Class* for The English Theatre, Frankfurt.

Katharine Williams
Lighting Designer

Katharine began her design career lighting in-the-round youth theatre productions at the Stephen Joseph Theatre, as well as in temporary venues at the National Student Drama Festival and the Edinburgh Fringe. She has subsequently designed lighting for some of the UK's most exciting emerging artists, as well as with established companies including Traverse Theatre, Aldeburgh Music, the National Theatre of Scotland, the Royal Court Theatre and the Royal Opera House, she was also Lighting Designer on *Amgen : Broken* (Sherman Cymru). Katharine enjoys working in non-traditional theatre formats, designing for drama, dance, physical theatre, opera, music and circus in the UK and internationally.

Dyfan Jones
Composer/Musical Director

Dyfan trained at Kingston University and The Guildhall School of Music and Drama. He began working professionally in 1995 and has been a Composer, Musical Director and Sound Designer on over one hundred theatre productions. As a television composer he has written music for numerous drama, factual and light entertainment series.

Theatre
The Snow Tiger/Teigr yr Eira (Sherman Cymru); *Sky Hawk, Rape of the Fair Country* (2013 revival), *Humbug!, A Feast of Festive Fun, Flora's War, Thinking Out Loud, Tall Tales, Festen, Great Expectations, Yesterday, Twilight Tales, Drowned Out, Measure for Measure, A Midsummer Night's Dream, A Toy Epic, Grapes of Wrath, Tales from Europe, Tales from Small Nations, To Kill a Mockingbird, Y Fordaith Fawr, Rape of the Fair Country, Song of the Earth, Abigail's Party, Hosts of Rebecca, Y Mabinogi, The Way It Was, Home Front, Oh! What a Lovely War* (Clwyd Theatr Cymru); *Love & Money* (Waking Exploits); *Melltith yr Helfesia, Morfa, Halt! Who Goes There?, The Bankrupt Bride, Cyrano, The Princess and the Hunter, Halen yn y Gwaed, Melangell* (Theatr na nÓg); *Beyond Borders, Mimosa, No Other Day Like Today, Canrif/Century, The Magnificent Myths of the Mabinogi* (National Youth Theatre of Wales); *Jack and the Beanstalk* (Stafford Gatehouse Theatre); *Porth y Byddar* (Clwyd Theatr Cymru/ Theatr Genedlaethol Cymru); *Dyled Eileen, Spring Awakening, House of America, 2110/Yn Y Trên, Y Gofalwr/ The Caretaker, Esther* (Theatr Genedlaethol Cymru); *Cider With Rosie, Hirdymor, I'r Byw, Spam Man, Skylight* (Theatre West Glamorgan); *Bonansa, Y Groesffordd, Radio Cymru* (Dalier Sylw); *Amdani, Indian Country* (Sgript Cymru).

Film and Television
Soli and Mo (CITV/S4C and Al Jazeera); *Cwm Teg* (Dinamo Productions for S4C); *Abadas, Dragon's Eye, Children in Need, Close to You, Wales Yesterday, A Christmas in Clay, Belonging, Just Up Your Street, The Indian Doctor, Voices, Save Our World* (BBC); *Teulu, Iechyd Da!, Dim Ond Celf, 31/12/99* (S4C); *Pobol y Cwm* (BBC for S4C); *Jac yn y Bocs* (Opus for S4C); *Jara, Pam Fi Duw?, Bydd yn Wrol* (HTV/Carlton for S4C).

Mike Beer
Sound Designer

Mike started his career at the Sherman Theatre in 1986.

Designs include: *Desire Lines* (Sherman Cymru); *The Borrowers, Merlin* (Sherman Theatre Company); *Coasting, Treasure Island, Peter Pan* (Bristol Old Vic); *Branches, Coriolan/us, In Water I'm Weightless, The Radicalisation of Bradley Manning, A Provincial Life, The Passion, The Persians, Love Steals Us From Loneliness* (National Theatre Wales); *Tir Sir Gar, Deffro'r Gwanwyn* (Theatr Genedlaethol Cymru); *Peter Pan* (Qdos); *Babel* (Wildworks); *BFG* (Fiery Angel); *The Firework Maker's Daughter, Danny the Champion of the World* (Birmingham Stage Company); *Single Spies, Legal Fictions, The Importance of Being Earnest* (The Theatre Royal Bath); *Don Quixote* (West Yorkshire Playhouse); *Chase the Glowing Hours with Flying Feet* (Diversions Dance Company); *Great Expectations* (Aberystwyth Arts Centre).

Julia Thomas
Assistant Director

Julia originally trained as an actor at Drama Centre London and has made the transition to directing by undertaking a mentorship programme with Living Pictures Productions under the guidance of Elen Bowman.

Assistant Directing credits include: *Peter Pan* (Sherman Cymru); *Diary of a Madman* (Living Pictures Productions); *A Provincial Life* (National Theatre Wales); *High Society* (National Tour).

Directing credits include: *Karamazoo* (Coleg Sir Gar); *A Bridge to the Stars* (Llanelli Youth Theatre) selected for National Theatre's Connections Festival, Olivier Theatre. Julia is currently directing *Marsha* by Alan Harris which will premiere at the Capital Fringe Festival, Washington DC this July.

In developing this tale for the stage, it became clear that there are many Dorothy Squires. Everyone remembers this icon, on a different scale, in a different era, light and mood. She herself was the master of spinning her own (often contradictory) yarns. This piece is about a Dorothy of our own invention. A private Dorothy in hiding from the world. A Dorothy full of memories, hopes and regrets, who did what she had to do.

We've created our own many-splendoured Dorothy and hope you will too. We think Miss Squires would approve.

Pia Furtado, Director

SAY IT WITH FLOWERS

by **Meic Povey** and **Johnny Tudor**

CHARACTERS

OLD DOT

YOUNG DOT

MAISIE

FREDDIE

ROGER

EMILY

The text was correct at the time of going to press
but may have altered slightly during rehearsals.

ACT 1

Scene 1

A cacophony of sounds: an orchestra tunes up. Applause. Train station bustle; traffic.

Old Dot stands with a suitcase and black bin bag. She wears huge, diamanté-encrusted glasses.
She takes off her glasses. Her eyes are closed. She opens them and stares at a letter in her hand.

Maisie appears, with a bunch of purple tulips, looking around.

Old Dot considers her and the letter in turn. Maisie sees Old Dot and waves enthusiastically.

As Maisie comes over Old Dot closes her eyes. An orchestra strikes up. An audience applauds. Old Dot opens her eyes. Maisie is in front of her and presents her with the flowers.

Old Dot smiles graciously at her audience.

The orchestra and the audience are replaced by train station bustle and traffic.

Maisie picks up the suitcase and black bin bag. She gestures for Old Dot to follow.

SCENE 2

A drab, grubby, curtainless room. There are purple tulips everywhere; a gramophone; a pile of Dorothy Squires albums; old concert posters; scrapbooks; framed photos of Dorothy.

Maisie appears carrying the suitcase and the black bin bag.

MAISIE: Come in! Come in!

Old Dot appears carrying the purple tulips. She registers her new home.

MAISIE: At last! I've got you all to myself, and I can't quite believe it! I honestly can't! Had you told me a month ago that I'd be standing in the same room as . . . ! Well . . . ! Just look at me now – the talk of the entire village! The toast I should say! You know what people are like – so starstruck it's unbelievable! You wouldn't think they had lives of their own! When is she coming? When will we see her, touch her? Any chance of hearing her sing? In her own good time, I say to them! When she's ready to meet her public and not a minute sooner! Eight days a week I've been at it, this last month. Not that I mind; it's all been worth it. And, once you're settled in, we'll have a look at the itinerary I've put together. Don't be alarmed! It's well thought out, I'm not some amateur. I've planned it to the last detail – who we see, where we go, how the next few weeks will unravel in general. You see, Dot – may I

2

call you Dot, by the way? You see, people here, they have small lives; small ambitions. Something like this . . . An event like this, it really gets them going. Of course, it's not the first time we've been blessed with celebrity. They filmed part of *The Citadel*, with Robert Donat right here in the village. In the thirties it was; you'll probably remember. This very house . . . ! . . . Was almost chosen for the main setting – the doctor's surgery? But they chose a house down the road in the end. A case of 'This is the bed Henry the Eighth would have slept in had he not stayed in the pub across the road', ha, ha!

Pause.

MAISIE: You were saying?

Pause.

MAISIE: We can move stuff around if you like?

Pause.

Any changes, just say the word . . .

Pause.

Right! Top of our list – the Con. Club! The place to be seen. Lovely location. Nice lounge. Smashing performing area! Some nice people too . . . and they don't all vote Tory. I happen to know that for a fact. There's live music on Fridays and Saturdays; and they also have a

3

very popular talent spot? Open-mic thing, you know. I've done a turn or two there myself as it happens. Shown off my wares, as it were. Now don't look so surprised! You're not the only singer in the room.

Pause.

MAISIE: I expect you'll be wanting to get your head down.

OLD DOT: I won't be here long.

MAISIE: Oh!

OLD DOT: I'm very grateful to you of course, but it's only a temporary arrangement.

MAISIE: You're welcome to stay for as long as you like.

OLD DOT: I'm looking at property as we speak: Surrey; Kent. Saw one in Mayfair, a possibility.

MAISIE: Very grand! And everybody needs a decent place to put their feet up after a hard day's grind.

OLD DOT: Where are you? Co-op? Factory of some kind? No, I expect they're all closed. Valleys haven't really changed much, have they?

MAISIE: I have my own business! My own corner shop. Didn't I mention it in my letter?

4

OLD DOT:	I get so many.
MAISIE:	Yes, but . . . Mine was rather special, wasn't it? Or you wouldn't be here, would you?!
OLD DOT:	I've had many offers.
MAISIE:	Oh, I'm sure! That's why I'm so grateful; so grateful that I'm the chosen one.
OLD DOT:	It came down to eeny-meeny-miney-mo in the end.
MAISIE:	Is that all?
OLD DOT:	Do you have a curtain for that thing?
MAISIE:	Of course, of course, of course! Came back from the cleaners yesterday. Still in the bag.

Old Dot takes a couple of steps towards the window.

OLD DOT:	Can they see me from the road?
MAISIE:	It'll be up before you can say 'Open Sesame'!
OLD DOT:	Am I on show? Is that why you invited me?
MAISIE:	No, of course not! You had nowhere else to go.
OLD DOT:	I've just told you – that's not true at all.
MAISIE:	That's what they said in the papers!

OLD DOT: Ha! Do you always believe what the papers say?

MAISIE: That's what they said and I wasn't having any of it! My Dorothy? Homeless? No way!

Pause.

OLD DOT: You're a very kind soul, Maisie.

MAISIE: My pleasure entirely! And in a sense it's only proper that we're together. Kindred spirits, we are.

OLD DOT: Are we?

MAISIE: We're Welsh. We've had the same upbringing. We've had to struggle to get where we are. And of course . . . you're not the only singer in the room!

OLD DOT: Well . . .Wonderful.

MAISIE: No great shakes, mind, but I've covered nearly all your songs!

OLD DOT: . . . I'm flattered.

MAISIE: Now don't get me wrong! I'm not comparing myself to you – that would be ridiculous. Like comparing Prince Charles to Prince Charming! There's only one Dorothy Squires after all.

OLD DOT: I like to think so.

MAISIE:	Could have gone all the way! Had to pack it in though. Family.
OLD DOT:	Shame.
MAISIE:	Auditioned for *Opportunity Knocks*, I did. I was a gnat's hair away from the bosom of Hughie Green himself! Of course, Ron – my Ron – he thought I was off my rocker! And so did the kids. Took quite a bit of stick in school to be honest. Showbiz mum, all that.

Pause.

MAISIE:	Away in England they are. Don't see them much.
OLD DOT:	That's what children, families, do. Out of sight, out of mind. Saves you the heartache.
MAISIE:	Oh, I don't know. Do you think so? Isn't it circumstances?
OLD DOT:	No. Choice.
MAISIE:	Mine, they had to go, see. Work . . .
OLD DOT:	There's work and work. Dreams are different. That's why I left. Alright for some people, obviously.

Pause.

MAISIE:	I'll help you unpack.

Maisie opens the mouth of the black bin bag.

OLD DOT: That won't be necessary.

Maisie reveals a mink coat.

MAISIE: Oh! What have we here? May I?

OLD DOT: No, don't touch it!

MAISIE: Sorry!

OLD DOT: Rather expensive you see. Not off-the-peg Peacocks.

MAISIE: Of course, of course. I know exactly where it came from!

OLD DOT: You do?

MAISIE: A 'certain gentleman' gave it to you in California, U. S. of A. I do believe?

OLD DOT: How would you know that? Who have you been talking to?

MAISIE: No, nobody. Nothing like that. Haven't you realised yet that I'm your biggest fan in the whole world?

OLD DOT: There's stiff competition. More than one queen would lay claim to that crown.

MAISIE: That's as may be but I've got all the press cuttings and, not only do I know who gave you this coat, I feel as if I've been wearing it for most of my life!

OLD DOT: Press . . . Ruined my life.

MAISIE: Necessary evil though, journalists . . . ?

OLD DOT: What the hell do you know?

Pause.

Some people are always hungry for gossip and I was fair game.

MAISIE: Well, it had its compensations. You'd kill for something like this, wouldn't you?

OLD DOT: You can hang it up for me if you'd like. Wore it at the Ritz once, while taking tea with Barbara Cartland and Lord Mountbatten.

MAISIE: Oh, the glamour!

OLD DOT: Called him an old poof. He didn't seem to mind.

MAISIE: And didn't you wear it at the The Talk of the Town, in September nineteen seventy-three?! I know you did because I was there! Sat right behind Shirley Bassey and two seats away from Lonnie Donegan!

OLD DOT: Is there anything you don't know about me?

MAISIE: Very little!

9

OLD DOT: I beg to differ!

MAISIE: No? Listen to this – what if I told you, just to make you feel at home, I've painted your bedroom blue?

Pause.

Blue bedroom? House in Bexley? Ding-a-ling-ling!

OLD DOT: I changed it to gold.

MAISIE: Oh!

OLD DOT: You must've missed that.

MAISIE: Sorry! It doesn't have to be blue; I'm not married to it. Gold! I'll change it to gold! Gold's a nice colour!

OLD DOT: I won't be here long enough for it to worry me.

MAISIE: I was only trying to make you feel at home. Must have been awful for you, what happened. Losing Bexley. What memories!

OLD DOT: The world and his wife came to my parties in Bexley.

MAISIE: Oh, I know, Dot. I know!

OLD DOT: Always a full house.

MAISIE:	House! More like a castle . . .
OLD DOT:	A full life . . .
MAISIE:	Beautiful!
OLD DOT:	There was beauty there. Show house, really . . . until he killed it.
MAISIE:	Bugger. But good for a while . . . ?
OLD DOT:	Brilliant.
MAISIE:	Go on! What was he like? Go on! What was he really like?
OLD DOT:	That's for me to know and for you to guess!
MAISIE:	I don't have to guess! He was handsome . . .
OLD DOT:	I suppose . . .
MAISIE:	Devastatingly handsome!
OLD DOT:	Yes! Yes, I suppose he was . . .
MAISIE:	And entertaining, I imagine! The raised eyebrow? You must've been in stitches half the time!
OLD DOT:	We made love the first night we met! Firm body. Full of vim. No stopping him.
MAISIE:	Shame he had to cack on it all.

OLD DOT: Pardon?

MAISIE: His betrayal. I hope you don't mind me saying – like a dagger through the heart, it was. I wept for days. Why? When he had you? And with an Eyetie if you please! Disgusting!

OLD DOT: Every time I closed my eyes I could see that Italian whore on my bed; I could smell her. I'll get the last laugh though. A shag to a man is like taking a crap – it's soon forgotten. But they always come back for love. And, when he does, when he comes knocking . . . five fingers to God I'll slam that door right in his fucking face!

MAISIE: Oh!!

Maisie is shocked. Old Dot falters but quickly gathers.

OLD DOT: Thank you, Maisie, that'll be all. I'm sure I'll be fine. I'll call if I need anything.

Maisie leaves awkwardly.
Suddenly, Old Dot seems very tired and old. She grimaces slightly; places a hand gingerly on her lower belly.

OLD DOT: Christ.

She considers her surroundings.

OLD DOT: I'm back. Jesus fucking Christ.

SCENE 3

Young Dot, using a hairbrush as a mic. She is wearing a brown dress with a silver star woven into its front. Her younger brother, Freddie, is listening to her in awe and admiration.

YOUNG DOT: (*Sings*)
'I'm no millionaire
But I'm not the type to care
'Cause I've got a pocketful of dreams
It's my universe
Even with an empty purse
'Cause I've got a pocketful of dreams
I wouldn't take the wealth of Wall Street
For a road where nature trods
And I calculate that I'm worth my weight
In goldenrods
Lucky, lucky me I can live in luxury
'Cause I've got a pocketful of dreams.'

Freddie, who's been fighting it, sniffs and wipes away a tear. Young Dot is 'emotional' too but doesn't want to show it.

YOUNG DOT: Don't do that. You're upsetting my concentration.

FREDDIE: Wy'n ffaelu help! Sa'i isie i ti fynd. (I can't help it! I don't want you to go.)

YOUNG DOT: Stop it! That babble's for the tin works and chapel. It won't do for where I'm going.

FREDDIE: But it's the language of heaven!

YOUNG DOT: Be that as it may, do you seriously think Gracie Fields got to where she is today by speaking Welsh?

FREDDIE: Do they have chapels in London?

YOUNG DOT: Of course they do.

FREDDIE: And will you still be going to Sunday school?

YOUNG DOT: Well . . . I'll be busy for a while. But once I've made a name for myself. . .

FREDDIE: On your own?

YOUNG DOT: Me and my voice. That's all I've got, Freddie.

FREDDIE: What about the tin works? Good job! Steady wages. What more could anybody want? And what if this singing lark fails? We're ordinary people is all I'm trying to say.

YOUNG DOT: 'We're all in the gutter, but some of us are looking at the stars'. Do you know who said such a beautiful thing?

FREDDIE: Dada?

YOUNG DOT: No! Dada's too dull and angry. Oscar Wilde!

FREDDIE: I don't know him. Is he from our street?

YOUNG DOT: No! Look, I've done my stint at the tin works. I've paid my dues. I've got the scars to prove it!

FREDDIE: You know when Jesus gave food to all those people?

YOUNG DOT: Yes . . . ?

FREDDIE: Was it five fishes and two loaves – or the other way round?

YOUNG DOT: What do you want to know that for . . . ?!

FREDDIE: In case they ask.

YOUNG DOT: It's five loaves and two fishes. Not hard to remember.

FREDDIE: It might be when you're not sitting next to me. What did Jesus ride on when he went to Jerusalem – donkey or ass?

YOUNG DOT: Donkey! Why all the questions?

FREDDIE: Because you won't be there and I'll be scared!

YOUNG DOT: You think I won't be scared? Four pounds, that's all I've got in the world!

FREDDIE: You've got me.

YOUNG DOT: I can't take you and I don't know anybody in London – I don't even have a job!

FREDDIE: Don't go then!

YOUNG DOT: I have to! God – He put me in the wrong place, Freddie.

FREDDIE: Pleddy!

YOUNG DOT: No! No more 'Nena', no more 'Pleddy'.

FREDDIE: No more singing? (*Sings*)
                'Mi sy'n fachgen ieuanc ffôl
                Yn byw yn ôl fy ffansi
                Myfi'n bugeilio'r gwenith gwyn' . . .

YOUNG DOT: (*'Caught'*. *Sings*)
                . . . Ac arall yn ei fedi.'

                Don't be selfish! That's all over. I'll be getting
                paid to sing from now on. You should be
                happy for me, Freddie. No more sneaking
                around. No more lying to Dada. No more
                changing in a phone box. It'll be number one
                dressing rooms for me. I'm telling you,
                Freddie. Once I'm a big star, we'll all live the
                life of Riley forever!

FREDDIE: You really mean it?

YOUNG DOT: We'll have a big house with lots of servants . . .
                and a pool . . . and stables for the horses! And
                a snooker room for you and Dada – and a
                huge grand piano, the biggest you've ever
                seen!

FREDDIE: And we can sing again?

YOUNG DOT: Oh yes, there'll be a lot of singing! People will
                travel from afar to see me – to adore me – to
                worship the very ground I walk on.

16

FREDDIE: Can I ask you one more question?

YOUNG DOT: Go on.

FREDDIE: What's the difference between a donkey and an ass?

YOUNG DOT: How the hell do you expect me to know? I'm from Llanelli!

FREDDIE: Maybe . . . Maybe you could ask somebody when you get to London.

Young Dot laughs.

YOUNG DOT: Dere 'ma'r twpsyn! (Come here, you idiot!)

She embraces him.

SCENE 4

Old Dot is putting a record on the gramophone. It is the opening bit of her comeback concert at the Palladium in 1970. She 'mouths' Dorothy Squires' words on the record.

OLD DOT: 'I hope I remember it all . . .'

Maisie appears.

MAISIE: Palladium! Nineteen seventy! I was there, as Max Boyce used to say! I was one of the lucky few! Couldn't get a ticket for love nor . . . !

OLD DOT: Took fifteen curtain calls!

MAISIE: Totally unforgettable! The best day of my entire life.

OLD DOT: After, in my dressing room, I could hear them shouting my name in the street below.

MAISIE: What a swansong!

OLD DOT: 'Swansong'? I'm not finished yet!

MAISIE: No, of course not! It's not what I meant at all.

OLD DOT: Then what did you mean?

MAISIE: You have so much more to give. We old troupers – well – we never die, do we? Now –

I've already put the feelers out at the Con. Club. Talked to Vince the Vice. Vice-treasurer. There's quite a buzz, and we've only had you a few weeks!

OLD DOT: What have you told them?

MAISIE: Only that . . . we might go down one night – once you feel all settled in – and that you might oblige with a song or two?

Old Dot discreetly touches her throat.

MAISIE: Everybody's waiting.

OLD DOT: Well . . .

MAISIE: After all, what is Dorothy Squires without the song? A ship without a sail!

Pause.

OLD DOT: Well . . . It might serve as a useful trial run, but I've been thinking about something on a grander scale.

MAISIE: Oh my God! Are you saying . . . ? Are you saying 'full frontal comeback'?!

Old Dot takes a moment to consider her surroundings and Maisie.

OLD DOT: Yes, why not. Singing's always been my ticket out. And anyhow, it's what my public want.

MAISIE: Oh, Dot! I love you! I love you so much!

OLD DOT: Calm down! There's a lot to do. I'll get
                 Bunny Lewis to set something up for me.

MAISIE: Swansea Grand? The New at Cardiff?

OLD DOT: Dear me, no. Brighton. They worship me
                 there. But I won't take second billing, mind!
                 I'll not have them shove that nonsense my
                 way like they did at The Talk of the Town.
                 I'll have to routine a new act of course. I'll
                 call Ernie. Nicky on stick . . .

MAISIE: (*She doesn't know what it means*)
                 Nicky on stick! Brilliant!

OLD DOT: Get Duggie to make me a new gown! I wonder
                 if he's still alive?

MAISIE: Duggie Darnell! What a plonker, eh? Stuck in
                 a traffic jam, with a two thousand pound
                 dress in his lap!

OLD DOT: You do not take to the stage at the Palladium
                 wearing any old thing; with your arse hanging
                 out. My fans adore me, so . . .

MAISIE: We thought you'd never make an appearance!
                 Worse hour of my life. A theatre-full of people,
                 all on the verge of a nervous breakdown! Poor
                 Pete Murray had to patter for twenty minutes.
                 Dyin' on his arse, he was.

OLD DOT: The truth of the matter is this – Duggie was still working on it; he didn't want to face me with an unfinished article. Prick . . . Now listen – we must get this show on the road. I'll need a telephone.

MAISIE: Telephone's no problem! I'll get Steve Sparks to run a line as soon as he's out of hospital.

OLD DOT: Curtains?

MAISIE: Ah! Sorry, sorry . . . Consider it done.

OLD DOT: Publicist? Who are the good, local ones?

MAISIE: (*A little bewildered*)
I'll ask around.

OLD DOT: Telephone – Done that . . . Calling cards!

MAISIE: Dorothy Squires – singer!

Old Dot smiles.

OLD DOT: Xerox! That's a priority . . .

MAISIE: What?

OLD DOT: Rank Xerox, photocopier. I'll need to send out flyers, photos, press releases, invitations . . .

MAISIE: I'll see what I can do . . . Perhaps we can use the photocopier at the Post Office?

OLD DOT: That's no good to me. I'm not going out there, I need it here. Is this all too much for you? Sorry, I wasn't thinking . . .

MAISIE: Good God, no!

OLD DOT: Maybe I should advertise for a personal assistant; a pro.

MAISIE: Hey! Stop that! I'm up to it. Lead me to the water and I'll drink.

OLD DOT: Beautifully said.

MAISIE: Anything else?

OLD DOT: Yes, there is actually. Blues.

MAISIE: What?

OLD DOT: Purple Hearts?

MAISIE: Eh?

OLD DOT: Amphetamines. Speed! Can you get me some?

MAISIE: They're illegal!

OLD DOT: Purely medicinal! For the comeback. Don't you want to see me at my best?

MAISIE: Of course! But I don't know any drug dealers.

OLD DOT: Drug dealers?! My chemist at Bexley,
Mr Jenkins, he used to give me a handful on a
regular basis. Called them my 'dolly mixtures'.
Of course, if it's too much trouble . . .

MAISIE: I didn't say that! I'll . . . I'll ask Brynley's son.
He's always up to no good.

OLD DOT: Excellent.

MAISIE: Oh, Dot bach!

OLD DOT: What?!

MAISIE: I can't believe you're making a proper
comeback! Can I tell them at the Con. Club?
Can I? Can I release the whiff of white
smoke?

OLD DOT: Well, by all means . . .

MAISIE: What are you going to sing?

OLD DOT: I don't know yet . . .

MAISIE: What about . . . ! What about . . .

OLD DOT: I dunno! I haven't routined my act yet.

MAISIE: You could do the Billy Reid medley, or the
River medley. Both!

OLD DOT: All of them . . . ?

MAISIE: I've got it!

'For once in my life I have someone who
needs me
Someone I've needed so long
For once unafraid, I can go where life
leads me
And somehow I know I'll be strong
For once I can say this is mine . . .'

Maisie starts dancing to the song.
She grabs hold of Old Dot.

OLD DOT: No!

MAISIE: Yes, come on!

They dance together. Old Dot laughs, starts enjoying herself.
They cling to each other, laughing. But Old Dot is quite
exhausted.

OLD DOT: I'll have to get myself into shape. Wouldn't
want to let anybody down.

MAISIE: Good grief, how could you? Oh, I can't wait
to see their faces! Champing at the bit they
are, see . . .
Some are very insistent. Weaving all sorts of
elaborate lies just to be near you . . .

OLD DOT: Really?

Maisie hesitates, before deciding to test the water.

MAISIE: One of them even claims to be family!

OLD DOT: I have no family.

24

MAISIE: Don't worry, she won't get past me.

Old Dot reacts.

MAISIE: (*She is careful*)
            Calls herself Emily,

OLD DOT: I've told you! I have no family!
                You need to smarten yourself up.

MAISIE: Sorry?

OLD DOT: Have you had a long hard look in the mirror
                lately? When did you last invest in a full
                M.O.T?

MAISIE: Had my hair done at Phyllis' only a couple of
                weeks ago.

OLD DOT: Finger in a dyke. I'm talking overhaul. I'm
                sure you're quite the little star in your own
                backyard . . . But you'll be with me; my bag
                carrier. Do you understand?

MAISIE: Yes! Yes! What should I do?

OLD DOT: Everything. I had my tits done once. Reduced.
                You can't even see the join. Look?

MAISIE: No! No, you're alright.

OLD DOT: Come here. Look at your eyes. Where's the
                colour? Where's the life? Ugh! And your
                chops. Is lipstick rationed in this village?

MAISIE: I suppose I could make a bit of an effort. I will! I will! For you . . .

OLD DOT: No, no, no. For yourself.

MAISIE: What?

OLD DOT: In this world you've got to give 'em what they want. Make the women yearn to be you – make the men want to bed you. Make yourself irresistible, Hilda . . .

MAISIE: Who?

Party music creeps in.

OLD DOT: What's that music?

MAISIE: What music?

OLD DOT: I love that tune . . .

MAISIE: Are you OK?

Pause.

No response from Old Dot who is listening to the music.

I'll get on with it!

Maisie exits.

SCENE 5

A lavish party is in full swing. Young Dot is in the spotlight. Roger is watching her.

YOUNG DOT: (*Sings*)
'When you wanna say I love you
Say it with flowers
When you wanna say I miss you
Say it with flowers
For they have a language
All their very own
They can calm life's seas
When stormy winds have blown.
When you wanna say you're sorry
Say it with flowers
When you wanna say don't worry
Say it with flowers
For they can speak I know you will agree
That heaven created them for you and me . . .'

The song ends, party music continues.

ROGER: Great party! Do you come here often?

YOUNG DOT: Who writes your scripts . . . ?!

ROGER: Hollywood's finest. Hopefully. Eventually.

YOUNG DOT: You and two thousand others! You've got the
                face for it, I'll give you that. They don't like
                good-looking men in this country – you've

got to have a big nose and a wonky eye to
make it.

ROGER: Thank you!

YOUNG DOT: Don't get carried away. Two thousand others,
remember?

ROGER: Not if I get a leg-up.

YOUNG DOT: You sure that's not 'over'? What's your name?

ROGER: Roger. Would you like to dance?

YOUNG DOT: Give me one good reason why I should dance
with you.

ROGER: Because I don't have a big nose and a wonky
eye?

YOUNG DOT: My secretary, Hilda, tells me you're an actor.
So . . . what restaurant are you working in at
the moment?

Roger laughs. Young Dot smiles.

ROGER: May I sleep in the blue room tonight?

YOUNG DOT: Who told you that blue is my favourite
colour?

He moves to kiss her.

YOUNG DOT: Just a minute, buster! Who the hell do you
think you are?

ROGER: A nobody. But you're obviously interested or you wouldn't be asking in such a charming manner.

YOUNG DOT: Don't get clever with me!

ROGER: I wouldn't dream of trying.

YOUNG DOT: You're trying too hard, that's your trouble.

ROGER: But getting somewhere, don't you think? You could simply walk away – or, better still – you could show me the door.

YOUNG DOT: I'll show you the door! Vamoose, amigo! Get out!

ROGER: I will if you really mean it.

YOUNG DOT: Haven't I just said?!

ROGER: You certainly have. But you know what they say – 'no' means 'yes', 'yes' means take me from behind.

YOUNG DOT: Fuck you!

She lashes out. Roger laughs, and catches hold of her arm before her hand connects.

ROGER: Now you're getting it! That's exactly what I want you to do!

YOUNG DOT: Let me go!

ROGER: Not until you promise me you'll marry me
and give me lots of children!

YOUNG DOT: You must be joking!

ROGER: Alright, I'll go.

He releases her and steps back.

ROGER: Enjoy the rest of your life.

YOUNG DOT: No, you don't! You'll go when I tell you to!

Roger laughs. She grabs hold of him.

YOUNG DOT: When I say!

They are close now.

ROGER: Say it then.

YOUNG DOT: I will now – in a minute.

ROGER: I'm still here.

YOUNG DOT: Yes you are, so what are you waiting for?

ROGER: Is this what you want?

YOUNG DOT: Isn't it fucking obvious?

They kiss passionately.

SCENE 6

A track of Dorothy Squires singing 'On a wonderful day like today'.

DOROTHY SQUIRES: (*Track*)
> 'On a wonderful day like today
> I defy any cloud to appear in the sky
> Dare any raindrop to plop in my eye
> On a wonderful day like today . . .'

An all-singing, all-dancing love scene between Young Dot and Roger, during which love letters fall from the heavens.

SCENE 7

A telephone has been installed. Old Dot picks up the letters one by one, carefully, possessively. She takes one out of its envelope.

OLD DOT: (*Reading*)
        'Darling, My darling, Mine'.

Maisie enters. She has tarted herself up a bit. Old Dot puts the letter back in its envelope hurriedly.

MAISIE:	Oh! Had some post? Fan mail is it? Who are they from? Give us a squint!
OLD DOT:	No. They're personal.
MAISIE:	Ah . . . They're from him aren't they?
OLD DOT:	They could be.
MAISIE:	Go on!
OLD DOT:	You've improved!
MAISIE:	I have, haven't I?
OLD DOT:	Much better.
MAISIE:	Thank you. Ooo-hooo . . . ! I feel all complimented! Do you need a safe place to put those?
OLD DOT:	No. They're mine.

MAISIE:	As you wish. But I've read that he'd do just about anything to get his hands on those!

Old Dot presses the letters to her bosom protectively.

MAISIE:	Found you a photocopier. Bit old, but in full working order. Not unlike yourself, Dot. Ha, ha! Oh . . . and the Con. Club have finally given me a spot in a few weeks! Is that OK?

Pause.

	You will do it, won't you? There's quite a buzz in the village already!
OLD DOT:	What? How do people know about it? I didn't promise anything to anyone!
MAISIE:	You promised me! And you will do it, won't you? For me? You have to do it, Dot!
OLD DOT:	Do I fuck.
MAISIE:	Don't you want Roger to come and see you?

With a nod towards the letters.

OLD DOT:	Don't be absurd. He wouldn't turn up in a one-horse town like this. The **Talk** of the Town, yes . . . !
MAISIE:	You never know! I'll get on to the 'Echo' and the 'Western Mail' – get a bit of publicity

going . . . your first big concert in years! Of course he'd come.

OLD DOT: Would he? Would he, Maisie? Oh hell. It might be fun. And worth it . . . So why not?! Christ, why not . . . ?

MAISIE: Then you'll do it?

OLD DOT: I'll do it.

MAISIE: (*Hysterics*)

Thank God! We're on! They're going to love it!

Maisie exits. Old Dot imagines Roger's presence already.

OLD DOT: Well hello there! It's good to see you. I'm so glad you came . . .

SCENE 8

Young Dot is on stage at The Talk of the Town.

YOUNG DOT: Thank you! Thank you! I'd like to dedicate this song to somebody very special, who just happens to be in the audience tonight. Look to your left, love . . .

HECKLER: Divorce him, marry me, Dot!

YOUNG DOT: I'll pay you later. Come on, give him a round. Give him the clap he so richly deserves.

Laughter and applause.

Come see me after the show. If you dare. Dressing room number one.

YOUNG DOT: (*Sings 'Till'*).
'Till the moon deserts the sky
Till all the seas run dry
Till then I'll worship you
Till the tropic sun turns cold
Till this young world grows old
My darling, I'll adore you
You are my reason to live
All I own I would give
Just to have you adore me
Till the rivers flow upstream
Till lovers cease to dream
Till then I'm yours, be mine . . .'

35

At the end of the song, Roger appears with a bunch of flowers.

YOUNG DOT: Saying it with flowers, Rog?

ROGER: You were sensational tonight.

YOUNG DOT: Most nights. Or have you forgotten?

ROGER: First concert in a while . . . ?

YOUNG DOT: I pick and choose these days.

ROGER: Don't be insulted. Thought you could do with a little extra, just to tide you over.

He hands her a cheque. She takes it.

YOUNG DOT: Very generous . . .

ROGER: A gift!

YOUNG DOT: In lieu of services rendered?

ROGER: Two-way traffic, hopefully.

YOUNG DOT: What are you after?

ROGER: What do you think, darling?

YOUNG DOT: Call me that again. Put 'my' in front of it. Please . . .

ROGER: (*A beat*)
My darling.

YOUNG DOT: Oh, Roger. My love!

She embraces him. He has no choice but to reciprocate.

ROGER: Are we still friends?

YOUNG DOT: Friends . . . ? Of course. Forever.

ROGER: Only . . . There is one thing!

YOUNG DOT: What? Is it over between you two? Tell me it's over.

ROGER: We have children, how can it be?

YOUNG DOT: Then why are you here?

ROGER: My letters . . . I want them back; and the divorce. It's been long enough already, Dot. Come on.

YOUNG DOT: It'll cost you.

ROGER: You'll give it to me?

YOUNG DOT: No, but when I do it'll set you back fifty grand.

ROGER: We're living in sin. It's not fair on the children. And those letters . . .

YOUNG DOT: Oh yes. Roger, those letters. 'Darling Dot', 'My darling', 'Mine'. 'How I long to be in your arms'. 'To be loved by you'. 'As no other woman could ever love me'.

ROGER: That's no longer true.

YOUNG DOT: Well why do you want them then?

ROGER: They're mine.

YOUNG DOT: They're in my bottom drawer. Let me remind you of something: I had to face the flames of hell to rescue those.

ROGER: Wasn't it just a burning house?

YOUNG DOT: Don't be facetious! I risked my life. Why should I give them back to you?

ROGER: You can't put them in that book. They're my copyright.

YOUNG DOT: And our love? Your copyright too?

ROGER: It doesn't exist anymore.

YOUNG DOT: No?

She brandishes her engagement and wedding rings.

ROGER: After seven years apart? Doesn't mean a thing.

YOUNG DOT: In God's eyes.

ROGER: That makes two of you then.

YOUNG DOT: The law's on my side too, when it comes to conjugal rights, boyo. Just you wait and see.

ROGER: Look Dot, feelings change. They overwhelm you. Then they die. You shrug your shoulders and move on.

YOUNG DOT: Oooh – very poetic – for you.

ROGER: Third-rate actor, pin-up boy, parasite? What am I today?

YOUNG DOT: Gigolo!

ROGER: Never heard you complaining. But then the older woman never does, does she?

YOUNG DOT: Fuck off! Go back to your Italian whore!

In a rage, Young Dot rips up the cheque he gave her. She grabs the flowers and proceeds to pelt him with them. He fights back, or at least tries to restrain her.

YOUNG DOT: Cunt!

ROGER: Harridan!

She takes off her rings and throws them at him.

YOUNG DOT: I'll never ever give you a divorce, you whore-master! And you will never ever see those letters again! They're mine!

Roger leaves.

YOUNG DOT: You can't fucking leave. I love you!

Young Dot crumples to the floor in a flood of tears and heartbreak.

SCENE 9

The previous memory has impacted badly on Old Dot, who throws things around in her rage and frustration. She is stopped in her tracks by stomach pains. She crumples to the floor in agony.
The telephone rings, but Old Dot is in so much pain that she can't reach it. It stops ringing and the answerphone kicks in.

EMILY: (*Voice*)
Hello . . . it's Emily. Please answer if you're there.

Old Dot stares at the phone.

OLD DOT: Emily.

SCENE 10

Young Dot and Freddie.

FREDDIE: You will come, won't you?

YOUNG DOT: I hate funerals. You know I hate funerals, Pleddy. Look, I would come were it possible, of course I would.

FREDDIE: Your own mother; what could be more important?

YOUNG DOT: Don't be judgemental.

FREDDIE: Will you come to mine?

YOUNG DOT: Why, are you going to be dying soon?

FREDDIE: Would you notice?

YOUNG DOT: Listen to me: I've an important date in Brighton. I've hired a thirty-six piece orchestra and backing singers. I can't let my fans down . . .

FREDDIE: Easier to let your own down?

YOUNG DOT: Can we not make this about you managing me again? I had to fire you, Freddie – for both of us! You weren't cut out for showbiz. And being bitter about it is getting really

tiring, may I say. This is my job. It's what I
do. And anyway, Mammy won't know . . .

FREDDIE: I'll know.

YOUNG DOT: I expected – hoped – you'd understand. I mean,
you – of all people – know how important my
work is. We hate goodbyes in our family, Pleddy!

FREDDIE: No more 'Nena'. No more 'Pleddy'.

YOUNG DOT: Don't be silly, it's not the end of the world!
What do you want from me? No more
singing? 'Mi sy'n fachgen ieuanc ffôl . . . '

Freddie stays silent.

YOUNG DOT: Alright, have it your own way, Captain Cunt.

FREDDIE: Will you promise me something?

YOUNG DOT: Yes, of course. No! I don't know. Promise
what? Don't ambush me . . .

FREDDIE: Will you look after Emily, should anything
happen to me?

YOUNG DOT: What's going to happen to you?! What the
hell are you saying . . . ?

FREDDIE: Or will you avoid her too?

YOUNG DOT: I'm not avoiding anybody! I'm simply
honouring contractual obligations! Stop
being so bloody dramatic . . .

FREDDIE: Promise you'll be there for her . . . ?

YOUNG DOT: When I'm not on stage – of course!

FREDDIE: Of course! I wouldn't dream of my daughter coming between you and your career!

YOUNG DOT: Cheap and uncalled for.

FREDDIE: I mean it. But there's only the two of us left now, Dot.

YOUNG DOT: I know, Pleddy. I'll always love you.

FREDDIE: Emily and me.

YOUNG DOT: Oh.

FREDDIE: Sorry if we're a nuisance, but . . .

YOUNG DOT: Oh, fuck off.

FREDDIE: Don't leave it too late, Nena.

YOUNG DOT: I said fuck off!

Young Dot turns to have more of an argument but Freddie has already left.

Applause.

YOUNG DOT: (*Sings 'My Mother's Day'*)
      'The one I love will always be
      Forever in my memory
      For all the love she gave to me

This is my mother's day
Just like an angel, she was there
All joys and sorrows, she would share
Inside my heart, a place is there
This is my mother's day
I still remember when I was a kid
From all trouble she used to hide me
But now I'm out in this world, all alone
Yet I know she is there to guide me
Though all the years may come and go
I bless her name and proudly so
I want the whole wide world to know
This is my mother's day
God bless her and keep her, forever and ever
This is my mother's day . . .'

SCENE 11

Old Dot is doing the scales, warming up her voice. It's a struggle. The voice cracks on the higher notes. She panics.

OLD DOT: Please God, touch my throat tonight.

Old Dot is hit by stomach pains. Maisie appears, carrying the mink coat. She has now completely transformed herself into a copy of Dot. Old Dot does a double-take but the pain keeps her in check. She conceals the pain from Maisie.

MAISIE: Ready? Here you are. I'm so excited!

Maisie gives her the coat.

MAISIE: What's the matter? Get your skates on, girl – we're supposed to be there in twenty minutes!

OLD DOT: Those blues you promised me . . . any luck?

MAISIE: It's not as simple as buying a packet of Smarties you know! Anyway you won't need them, not tonight. The adrenaline will keep you going! I'm on overdrive already. Come on, let's go. Put your coat on . . .

OLD DOT: No, wait . . . I need them. If I'm to sing tonight, I need blues . . .

MAISIE: Well I'm sorry, but I haven't got any!

OLD DOT: Then I can't perform!

MAISIE: What are you on about?

Pause.

No. Don't tell me that. The whole village is out. How could you disappoint them? Disappoint me?

OLD DOT: Disappoint? It's only the Con. Club for heaven's sake! Hardly the Palladium.

MAISIE: To you, maybe! I live here and every single ticket has been sold. What do I tell them? What will I tell Vince the Vice when he looks me in the eye? Is it your voice?

OLD DOT: My voice?

MAISIE: That sore throat you had the other day?

OLD DOT: Nothing wrong with my throat. Don't you fucking dare say there is!

MAISIE: Well what then?! Our big night and you go and spoil it.

OLD DOT: No, Maisie – your big night!

MAISIE: You agreed!

OLD DOT: You bullied me! Me – Dorothy Squires – performing to a few piddling Tories in the back of beyond? Why should I bother with that?

MAISIE: Because you never let your audience down.

OLD DOT: Your audience. You do it.

Pause.

MAISIE: Don't be ridiculous!

OLD DOT: Yes. It would be ridiculous.

MAISIE: Well, I have no choice, if you're going to let everybody down.

OLD DOT: Don't be a berk. I was only joking.

MAISIE: No joke for me. They're expecting a bona fido legend and that's what they're going to get.

OLD DOT: You?!

MAISIE: I won't disappoint them. Gimme that coat.

Maisie grabs the coat.

OLD DOT: But you can't sing!

MAISIE: Can you?

Maisie exits.
Old Dot clutches her belly. She is delirious.

OLD DOT: Beware of the band leader, Maisie! One minute, you're a little dwt singing in the choir

and the next, you're backstage in Clacton,
spread out on a skip, waiting to go on. He's
heaving, sweating, smells of booze . . .

SCENE 12

Young Dot is being 'seduced' whilst waiting to go on stage.

YOUNG DOT: Are you using a letter? You'd better be 'cos sure as heck music and babies don't go. No, no. Of course you're safe as houses, Billy. Will they like me tonight? I know that I'm new to the game but am I doing well?

Pause.

You know I was the littlest kid in the choir. The short-arse with all the grown-ups. I had such beautiful clothes. Dada loved me in my beautiful clothes, but he would never let me have shoes. Oh no. Always boots. I was a fairy with little white boots, and the stage was made of railway sleepers and it sounded like a xylophone when you walked on it.

OLD DOT: He doesn't say he loves you for all of that. You hear the overture; he wipes his cock on a hanging black. You go on, ignoring what might be baking in your belly. And it's the best performance of your life . . .

VOICE: Beginners. Beginners call, ladies and gentlemen. Miss Squires to the stage.

YOUNG DOT: (*Sings, 'I'm Walking Behind You'*)
'I'm walking behind you
On your wedding day

And I'll hear you promise
To love and obey
Though you may forget me
You're still on my mind
Look over your shoulder
I'm walking behind
Maybe I'll kiss again
With a love that's new
But I shall wish again
I was kissing you
'Cos I'll always love you
Wherever you go
And though we are parted
I want you to know
That if things go wrong, dear
And fate is unkind
Look over your shoulder
I'm walking behind . . .'

SCENE 13

Old Dot doubles over in pain.

OLD DOT: Torn from my belly. The show must go on.

A ghostly Freddie appears.

FREDDIE: How can it go on when you're ill.

OLD DOT: I'm not ill. I'm fine.

FREDDIE: Na, dwyt ti ddim. (No, you're not)

OLD DOT: Yes I am.

FREDDIE: Wy'n dy garu di, Nena. (I love you, Nena)

OLD DOT: I don't understand.

FREDDIE: Wrth gwrs dy fod ti. (Of course you do) Why are you lying to yourself?

OLD DOT: I'm not! That language is dead to me. You're dead!

FREDDIE: All neb osgoi 'u gorffennol. (Nobody can escape their past)

OLD DOT: Jesus Christ!

FREDDIE: We're all watching you. Mama, Dada, me. Nobody can escape their past.

OLD DOT: They're dead. You're dead.

FREDDIE: Emily.

Freddie disappears.

SCENE 14

Old Dot takes stock. She feels terribly alone – and a little afraid. She goes to the telephone and dials.

EMILY: (*Voice*)
                    Emily Squires . . . Hello?

Old Dot hesitates.

EMILY: (*Voice*)
                    Hello?

Old Dot puts the receiver down.

END OF ACT I

ACT II

SCENE 1

A photocopier has been installed. Old Dot is busy and focused. There are song sheets and newspaper clippings strewn all over the room. She's in some pain but determined.

A knock on the door. Old Dot waits. Silence. Old Dot becomes slightly anxious.

Another knock. Old Dot smiles to herself.

OLD DOT: Come!

Maisie enters awkwardly. She has a bag of fish and chips.

OLD DOT: Well, look who's here! She lives – she breathes – Miss Rhondda Valley, nineteen-ninety!

MAISIE: I've . . . brought you a bit of supper.

OLD DOT: I see – decided to grace me with your person, rather than leave it by the door like a dog's dinner? You needn't have bothered. I've managed perfectly, these last few days. Did you think I wouldn't? Did you think I'd keel over and die without you?

MAISIE: I'll take it away.

OLD DOT: Leave it! Waste not, want not and all that.

MAISIE: It's just cod and chips, mind.

Maisie allows herself a small, satisfied smile. She hands Old Dot the package. Old Dot tucks in ravenously.

OLD DOT: So . . . how did it go the other night?
                Standing-room only at the Con. Club?

MAISIE: I see you've got the photocopier . . . ! Nice,
                innit? Brynley got it at a knock-down price!
                Is it working OK . . . ?

OLD DOT: It does the job.

MAISIE: Been busy . . . ?

OLD DOT: Busy! Like the proverbial blue-arsed fly!
                Thank God I've the energy of a woman half
                my age! Not that I'd particularly want to be
                half my age again, you understand. Youth is
                overestimated, don't you think? No, I wouldn't
                want the old days back – not with the thunder
                in me now!

MAISIE: What exactly have you been doing?

OLD DOT: Publicity drive! Sending out invitations and
                'save the dates'! All the societies and
                establishments that adore me in Brighton and
                the surrounding area! I need to inform my
                fans that I'm on my way – get the gays firing
                on all cylinders!

MAISIE: Right . . . So the Brighton concert is still a
                goer?

OLD DOT: Of course! Did you think I was not going to do it?

MAISIE: (*Pointed*)
People do change their minds.

OLD DOT: I see; we're back to the Con. Club are we? Oh, dear – you really are one of them, aren't you?

MAISIE: Who?

OLD DOT: Those unfortunates you mentioned. You know – small lives, small ambitions.

MAISIE: Alright! Alright . . . I'm sorry it went pear-shaped. It all got out of hand.

OLD DOT: Yes, you did, didn't you? Very emotional!

MAISIE: I shouldn't have taken your coat . . . !

OLD DOT: Is that all?

MAISIE: Sorry!

OLD DOT: Took my mantle, no less! Or tried to. But – when push came to shove – did you cut the mustard, that's the question?

MAISIE: Don't be like this. I've been dead worried, I have! Brynley told me you looked quite pale – decidedly under the weather, he said.

OLD DOT:	Doctor of medicine, is he? If you were so worried, why didn't you call in to see me?
MAISIE:	You should've called me if you were unwell! Phone does work, doesn't it? It must do, if you've been calling Brighton non-stop!
OLD DOT:	Who said I'd been doing that?
MAISIE:	Call anyone in particular in Brighton these last few days? (*Beat*) Emily . . . ?
OLD DOT:	I might have . . .

A look.

MAISIE:	I think you have. See, she called me again, earlier . . .
OLD DOT:	I need you to do something for me!
MAISIE:	Said you've been phoning – but not speaking, and ringing off.
OLD DOT:	She always was a little liar.
MAISIE:	So why are you bothering with her?
OLD DOT:	Never mind her. That particular train left the station a long time ago.

Maisie smiles.

OLD DOT:	Shift your arse over here, you. Have a gander at these . . .

Old Dot has produced a dozen or so pieces of fine-looking jewellery.

MAISIE: Good grief! Where did you get these?

OLD DOT: Where do you think? I'm La Squires – part and parcel of the legend.

MAISIE: You never told me you had these with you!

OLD DOT: I've never told you I'm having difficulty pissing, but there you go.

MAISIE: They're beautiful!

OLD DOT: Fifteen grand's worth. At auction – collector's items – maybe more.

MAISIE: You're selling them . . . ?!

OLD DOT: I need money. Brighton won't go away. My fans expect. Get me Sotheby's number, there's a good girl.

MAISIE: I don't know. Isn't there another way? (*She handles a piece*) Pity to see 'em go . . .

OLD DOT: It'll be a nice day out for us – Sotheby's, Selfridges . . . take in a show.

MAISIE: Tea at the Ritz!

OLD DOT: That's the idea. Now, have a look at this one!

Old Dot hands Maisie a delicate ankle chain with inscription.

OLD DOT: Read the inscription. Go on, read it aloud.

MAISIE: 'I love you'. Ah . . . !

OLD DOT: Given that by Roger. Proof positive.

MAISIE: And this is going too?

OLD DOT: Afraid so!

MAISIE: But . . . ! Don't you wish you could . . . pass them down? To the next generation, so to speak? Your legacy, like? I know I'd want to . . . !

OLD DOT: Naturally. You have family.

MAISIE: You have family, Dot. Emily. No point denying it. But I'd totally understand why you wouldn't want to give them to her!

OLD DOT: Exactly! Is she here now? My fans are my family. You are, Maisie. In fact, you're my next of kin.

MAISIE: (*Simply*)
    Oh Dot. I love you.

OLD DOT: Never mind that. Come on – tell me . . . how did it go? Did you tear the bollocks off 'em at the Con. Club?

MAISIE: I wish! It wasn't the talking I minded so much – it was the laughter that killed. Won't be able to show my face in the village for months!

OLD DOT: Oh, stop feeling sorry for yourself, for goodness' sake! We've all had the carpet swept out from under out feet, at one time or another. Life goes on. Don't let the buggers get you down.

MAISIE: I feel bad for them, to be honest. They didn't get you – didn't get to hear your wonderful voice.

OLD DOT: That's why we must get on with Brighton, may I say.

Then it hits Old Dot – pain; terrible pain.

OLD DOT: Fuck! Christ! Cunt!

MAISIE: Wassa matter?! Wassa matter?! Oh Dot bach, you've got to see a doctor!

OLD DOT: There's nothing wrong with me!

MAISIE: Let me make an appointment with Dr Chaudri in the village!

OLD DOT: No! You get me some blues! Get me some fucking blues and I'll be right!

MAISIE: Blues won't help this!

OLD DOT: Don't just stand there! Haven't I given you things to do?! Go! Out! Out!

Old Dot bundles Maisie out.

Maisie knocks on the door, trying to get back in.

Old Dot resumes photocopying, ignores Maisie.

A cacophony of sound. Through the photocopier and applause we hear Young Dot singing a phrase of 'Your Flowers Arrived Too Late'.

SCENE 2

Emily knocks. Young Dot is at the piano.

YOUNG DOT: Come in!

EMILY: New song for your act?

YOUNG DOT: Just fiddling . . . How are you settling? Happy?

EMILY: Yes, Auntie Dorothy! Very happy. I'll always be so grateful to you . . . !

YOUNG DOT: Well, somebody had to rescue you from the clutches of those evil lesbian nuns!

Emily gasps in mock outrage.

YOUNG DOT: Look after your own, Emily, and the rest will look after itself.

EMILY: Daddy sends his love.

YOUNG DOT: When did you last see your mother?

EMILY: She's on tour with Max Miller.

Pause.

Coming up to three months. Poor Mum!

YOUNG DOT: Poor Max Miller!

EMILY: I'm sorry . . . ?

YOUNG DOT: Only joking! I'm so glad you're with me now, Em. We're going to have the time of our lives! You won't let me down will you?

EMILY: Of course not! Why would you say that . . . ?

YOUNG DOT: You won't be in a hurry to leave, I mean. This house is dead without people. Not that I'd stop you!

EMILY: Why would I go?

YOUNG DOT: Where would you go? You can hardly traipse around the country with Joyce and Mr Miller!

Emily laughs nervously.

EMILY: If I could, I'd live here forever!

YOUNG DOT: The house is big enough – we won't get in each other's way.

EMILY: Plenty of bathrooms!

YOUNG DOT: More mirrors than the Moulin Rouge! What more could two young women want?

Emily giggles.

EMILY: Well . . . !

YOUNG DOT: What?

EMILY: No. Nothing!

YOUNG DOT: Go on! What do you want?

EMILY: It's embarrassing, Auntie Dorothy!

They laugh.

YOUNG DOT: Go on.

EMILY: A boyfriend . . . hopefully!

YOUNG DOT: OK! We'll see what we can do!

EMILY: Ok!

YOUNG DOT: Of course, you'll have to have a complete makeover . . . Who's your hairdresser? Should be shot.

EMILY: Auntie Dorothy . . . !

YOUNG DOT: And that outfit . . . ! I'll find you a decent couturier . . .

Emily giggles.

YOUNG DOT: I'm serious. We'll get you looking gorgeous. But listen here – you be careful with men.

EMILY: Where's the man of the house?! Will Uncle Roger be home soon? I can't wait to see him! Where is he at the moment?

YOUNG DOT: Zagreb.

EMILY: That's in Yugoslavia!

YOUNG DOT: Apparently.

EMILY: What's he doing there?

YOUNG DOT: Who's he doing more like.

EMILY: What . . . ?

YOUNG DOT: A film! Something . . .

EMILY: When will he be home? Will I get to see him this summer? Is he still doing *The Saint*?! Da ra da da da ra da! (*Theme tune to TV series 'The Saint'*)

She draws a 'halo' above her head.

YOUNG DOT: Let me tell you something, Emily – I could get any man on the planet – any man I wanted.

EMILY: Bet he could get any woman!

Young Dot grabs her and gives her a good shake.

YOUNG DOT: You take that back, you little bitch! I'm sorry! Oh, darling, I'm so sorry! Come here. Come to Mummy!

Young Dot tries to embrace Emily – but Emily pushes her away.

EMILY: You're not my mother!

YOUNG DOT: Don't say that! Who's looking after you? I love you, Em.

EMILY: I don't understand. We were only talking . . .

YOUNG DOT: Stop putting him on a pedestal. Roger's not the be all and end all of my life. No man should ever be. You hear?

EMILY: Not even Daddy?

YOUNG DOT: Let's not talk about this . . .

EMILY: He's a man . . . !

YOUNG DOT: My brother! Different. Look, don't upset yourself all over again.

EMILY: He really wants to see you. He doesn't get out much these days.

YOUNG DOT: Well, tough. I'm really busy. My schedule's just impossible these days.

EMILY: I don't get it – why can't you two work it out?

YOUNG DOT: It's not from want of trying on my part, believe me! He's still bitter. Blames me for sacking him. I needed a dynamic manager, not some kid hanging on my apron strings! That's showbiz – and your father couldn't hack it!

EMILY: Is that it? All this over a job? A stupid job?!

YOUNG DOT: Look, are we going to have fun, or are we going to make ourselves miserable by picking at the scab?!

EMILY: He's family! Isn't that what it's all about? Isn't that why I'm here? 'Look after your own', isn't that what you said a minute ago?

YOUNG DOT: Now that's enough! Enough of this . . . this interrogation! Don't keep going on at me. Don't be like your father.

SCENE 3

Old Dot's in pain. Ghostly Freddie appears.

FREDDIE: Family come first.

OLD DOT: Christ, not you again.

FREDDIE: Not feeling well, Nena?

OLD DOT: No. I'm fine. Lead me to the stage. Once I hit
the boards, Dr Footlights will see me right.

FREDDIE: Why won't you admit you're ill?

OLD DOT: (*Sings, as loud as she can*)
'Pack up your troubles in your old kit bag
and smile, smile, smile . . . !'

FREDDIE: (*Sings louder*)
'And now the end is near, and so I face the
final curtain . . .'

OLD DOT: Shut up!

FREDDIE: (*Sings*)
'My friends I'll make it clear, I'll state my
case of which I'm certain . . .'

OLD DOT: Shut up! Shut up! Shut up!

*Maisie appears, in time to see Old Dot throw a small projectile
in the general direction of Freddie. Maisie cannot see or hear him.*

MAISIE: What's all this?! What in God's name are you doing . . . ?!

FREDDIE: Tell her, Nena. Tell her the truth.

OLD DOT: (*To Freddie*)
You shut up! (*To Maisie*) Nothing!

MAISIE: Now you listen to me, goo' girl – I've just about had enough of this! You're going to see Dr Chaudri whether you like it or not. You've got to see somebody!

FREDDIE: Face it, Nena.

OLD DOT: (*To Freddie*)
When hell freezes over!

MAISIE: You must! I don't want to be left holding the baby should anything happen to you!

OLD DOT: (*Caressing her painful belly*)
My baby! My baby!

MAISIE: What the hell are you going on about? You don't have a baby.

FREDDIE: Don't worry, Nena. Dr Footlights will see you right.

OLD DOT: Fuck off!

MAISIE: Don't you tell me to fuck off! I'm trying to help you before it's too late!

FREDDIE: You'll have to face the final curtain.

OLD DOT: Curtains! That'll be the day!

MAISIE: Yes, I'd better get around to it soon as I can. Nobody wants to see this!

OLD DOT: Christ! (*A spasm of pain*) Call BUPA.

FREDDIE: Too grand for the village doctor.

OLD DOT: My husband will pay. He's a millionaire.

MAISIE: Will he buffalo! Get real, for pity's sake!

FREDDIE: Take a good look at yourself.

OLD DOT: I told you to fuck off!

She grabs hold of a wine glass and throws it at Freddie. Maisie is frightened and leaves hurriedly.

SCENE 4

*Old Dot's hand is bleeding. Roger appears. Old Dot is still
hallucinating.*

ROGER: You can't keep smashing into our lives like
this.

OLD DOT: So restrain me.

ROGER: Your hand's bleeding.

OLD DOT: It's my heart that's bleeding. Make it better,
Rog. Let's fall in love – get married again –
have lots of children.

ROGER: Will you carry them?

OLD DOT: Trust me.

ROGER: Too late. Louisa's a natural born mother.

OLD DOT: That's not love, that's lust.

ROGER: You only get rid of them.

OLD DOT: No, no, no . . .

ROGER: Abort.

OLD DOT: With Billy! Took my virginity, left me the
song.

ROGER: But it was all about the Song, Dot – don't you remember?

OLD DOT: 'I hope I remember it all . . .'

ROGER: The Song came first.

OLD DOT: If I could wish upon a star I'd trade it all for the patter of tiny feet. The feeling of it baking. My belly kicking. Hurting. Hurting so much. It has to come out. Had to come out. Billy's child, not yours. I want ours, Rog. We made love until dawn . . . The night you gave me this.

Old Dot brandishes the ankle chain.

OLD DOT: All I had on. Look away, you naughty boy! Patience.

She lifts her skirt up a bit. She attempts to bend down, in order to fasten the chain around her ankle. She cannot reach.

OLD DOT: Fucking skirt!

She hikes the skirt up. There is a catheter attached to her leg.

OLD DOT: Oh . . . ! Don't worry about this, Rog. It won't come between us. Normal service will be resumed. Come here. Say you love me. Kiss me.

The telephone rings. Old Dot looks at the phone.
Roger disappears.
The answerphone kicks in.

EMILY: (*Voice*)

Hello? Are you there? Please pick up, Auntie Dorothy! Speak to me!

Freddie appears.

FREDDIE: Why won't you speak to her?

OLD DOT: Where's Roger? He was about to give me a tumble . . . What have you done with him?! This may be my last chance . . .

FREDDIE: It is your last chance. Don't you want to say goodbye?

OLD DOT: Why should I? She betrayed me. Left me to the wolves. They all did.

FREDDIE: No she didn't. She stood up to you because she loved you. She dared to love you, Nena. You couldn't handle an honest broker. You couldn't face the truth. And you still can't.

OLD DOT: Where was her love when I needed it most?

SCENE 5

Young Dot is anxious; on edge. Emily arrives.

EMILY: Hello, Auntie Dorothy. Sorry I'm late.
                David's recording session went over.

YOUNG DOT: Never mind. No one followed you, did they?

EMILY: No.

YOUNG DOT: Press everywhere.

EMILY: How are you?

YOUNG DOT: Oh, you know!

EMILY: A bit apprehensive . . . ?

YOUNG DOT: Ha! Putting it mildly. Still with that David then?

EMILY: Give him a chance, Auntie Dorothy. He loves
                me. And he's going to leave his wife soon . . .

YOUNG DOT: Of course he is. They all say that.

EMILY: He really is.

YOUNG DOT: Stop trusting men, Em. Makes you look like
                a fool.

EMILY: I want you to be pleased for me, Auntie
                Dorothy – happy . . .

YOUNG DOT: Happy! How the fuck can I be happy about anything, with this . . . this sword of Damocles hanging over me?

EMILY: That was thoughtless of me . . . Who's coming with you to court? I will if you like. I know the drill.

YOUNG DOT: (*An opportunity*)
Would you? Would you really, Em? (*She pauses*) You see . . . It's all just a ghastly mistake.

EMILY: All I know is what I've read . . .

YOUNG DOT: In 'The News of The World'? Don't trust a word. That bastard Murdoch's been out to get me since he made up all that crap about Roger. Love turns sour, my arse. When this is over, I'll sue him again! And I'll win again too. You know they're saying I bribed Jack Dabbs?! You remember Jack, don't you?

EMILY: That creepy producer off *Family Favourites*?

YOUNG DOT: That's the one. They're claiming I paid for his hotel in exchange for him playing my records on his radio programme. It's ridiculous!

EMILY: And did you?

YOUNG DOT: They're all at it! I was just plain unlucky! The cunt even had the nerve to put his fags on the bill.

EMILY: So you did pay his bill . . . ?

YOUNG DOT: No, no, no, no . . . Yes, I paid because they wouldn't take his cheque. He's a friend! I paid in cash . . . and Jack refunded the money – in cash – once we returned to England.

EMILY: Then you've nothing to worry about.

YOUNG DOT: My word against theirs, unfortunately. What are we gonna do? You see, Em . . . what I need – what I desperately need – is for somebody to back my version of events – to say they witnessed the transaction. Someone I can trust– who trusts me . . .

EMILY: But, if it was just the two of you, how's that going to work?

YOUNG DOT: You were there.

EMILY: No, not in Gibraltar. In Malta, the year before . . .

YOUNG DOT: Same thing . . .

EMILY: Sorry . . . ?

YOUNG DOT: A small adjustment.

EMILY: But it's not, is it? I wasn't there.

YOUNG DOT: Will you do it?

EMILY: You mean . . . take the stand? Lie on oath?

YOUNG DOT: You wouldn't be lying! It's all a misunderstanding.

EMILY: So, to be clear, you'd have me lie for you – your own blood?

YOUNG DOT: There, you said it. Blood! You'd be doing it for the family. It's what families do.

EMILY: Families do funerals too.

YOUNG DOT: Christ! Not this again! Get over it, Emily – he's been dead for five years. I don't need him getting at me from beyond the grave, now!

EMILY: It's you that's talking about family and you still haven't told me – why weren't you there?

YOUNG DOT: I was probably working!

EMILY: No surprises there then.

YOUNG DOT: I need you to do this for me.

EMILY: No, it isn't right!

YOUNG DOT: There are no rights or wrongs, my girl – only opinions!

EMILY: Maybe for you – I know this is wrong.

YOUNG DOT: Then you'll betray me.

EMILY: Betray? No! But I won't lie on oath; not even for you.

YOUNG DOT: Fuck off, then. And you can move your stuff out of my house while you're at it.

EMILY: That's your answer to everything, isn't it? Push it away. Ignore it. Just like you did with Daddy.

YOUNG DOT: For fuck's sake. Don't you understand? If I don't beat this wrap, I'm finished. Dorothy Squires! Over! That's why they're out to get me! They're all at it out there, but they're picking on me! Do you realise what's going on here? It's corruption, Emily! Up there with . . . with perjury and perverting the course of justice! It's not a parking ticket! We're talking needle and thread – we're talking mailbags!

EMILY: Prison? Don't be dramatic. It won't come to that!

YOUNG DOT: What do you know? They're out to get me – ruin me, pull me down . . . I can't think about the damage it will do to my reputation. I won't be able to face anyone. There'll be no point in carrying on.

EMILY: You'll bounce back, Auntie Dorothy! You always do. Tore the bollocks off 'em at the Palladium, didn't you? New album? New fans? You have thousands of loyal fans out there! They won't desert you.

YOUNG DOT: Mary, mother of fucking Christ, do I have to spell it out for you? If I go down, the BBC

won't touch me ever again. If they don't hear
my songs on the airwaves I'll be playing to
empty theatres!

EMILY: It's only your job!

YOUNG DOT: Job?! I've sacrificed everything for this. The
airwaves are my oxygen – my life blood . . .
Without it what have I got? Tell me. What?
And you're going to rip it away from me!

EMILY: How dare you?! This has nothing to do with
me. It's you that's messed up. I'm just being
honest.

YOUNG DOT: Oh yes! Stand there on your high horse, just
like your father, while they tear me to pieces.

EMILY: The world isn't all about you! There are
bigger things. I'm trying to be honest with
you! I'm giving you some truth. Somebody
has to . . .

YOUNG DOT: Fuck your honesty! I need your help!

EMILY: I've said no!

YOUNG DOT: Well you're no fucking good to me then. I
don't want to see your face around here
again!

SCENE 6

Old Dot is hallucinating.

YOUNG DOT: Get out of my sight!

OLD DOT: Go on, fuck off!

YOUNG DOT: I've looked at my brother's face for too long!

Emily disappears.

OLD DOT: You have to live with that, you ungrateful bitch!

Freddie appears.

OLD DOT: What do you want?

FREDDIE: You got to come right away, Nena.

OLD DOT: Why? What for?! I'm not coming with you!

Roger appears.

FREDDIE: You know what for, Dot.

ROGER: You've broken the law.

OLD DOT: No, I haven't!

ROGER: You're guilty of corruption.

OLD DOT: No, I'm not!

ROGER: Don't lie. Careful what you say, Dot. You can make it better if you just come.

OLD DOT: I haven't done anything!

Old Dot comes face-to-face with Young Dot. They look.

OLD DOT: Christ!

YOUNG DOT: I wouldn't go with them, Edna May. It's the beginning of the end.

OLD DOT: That's rich coming from you. You got me into this mess.

YOUNG DOT: All I did was fight for us. Look where it got us. The state of you!

OLD DOT: Then you should've topped yourself, years ago!

YOUNG DOT: Couldn't. The Song.

OLD DOT: Oh yes. The Song. Not much song left now, is there?

YOUNG DOT: Fight. You're a fighter. Fight for the Song!

OLD DOT: What if I don't want to? I'm tired.

YOUNG DOT: Who are you? You're not Dorothy Squires . . . You're just an old woman.

OLD DOT: I am Dorothy Squires! I am . . . I am . . .

YOUNG DOT: You're scaring me.

OLD DOT: I'm scared. What's going on?

YOUNG DOT: You'd better deal with it.

OLD DOT: It's your doing. You can't leave.

ROGER: (*As policeman*)
Come with us, please, Miss Squires.

YOUNG DOT: It's not me you want, it's her!

Young Dot exits.

ROGER: Are you Dorothy Squires?

OLD DOT: Yes! But I'm innocent! Get your fucking filthy hands off me. Hang about . . . Rog? Whose side are you on?

Maisie appears.

MAISIE: Yours, Dot. Always.

OLD DOT: Where are they taking me? Prison? I haven't done anything. Let me go!

MAISIE: Hospital.

OLD DOT: What for? I thought you were arresting me?

ROGER: Please be still. We don't want to have to restrain you.

OLD DOT: You can't do this to me. My arse is on the line here. My career. My life.

MAISIE: Your piss is playing havoc with your insides, Dot! Infection it is, see . . .

OLD DOT: The establishment is infected. That's why you're doing this to me. Payola? Bollocks.

FREDDIE: Face it, Nena. It's cancer. You won't beat this wrap.

OLD DOT: Fuck off, Freddie.

MAISIE: She's delirious see, Doctor. Doesn't know who we are!

ROGER: You are being arrested on charges of corruption, Miss Squires. How do you plead?

OLD DOT: Not guilty. It's only a haematuria.

EMILY: (*Masked*)
Let me explain, Miss Squires. You've got an infection. Catheter maintenance needs to become part of your daily routine . . .

OLD DOT: Yes! I need to routine a new act. Yes, I know. I'll call Ernie. Get Nicky on stick . . .

FREDDIE: We can help you. We're all here, Nena. Watching you. Mammy, Dada, me . . .

MAISIE: You want to be on top form for your comeback, don't you?

OLD DOT: Comeback? Yes . . . yes, I do. It'll be like the second coming. Even better than the Palladium. Packed to the rafters. My thousands of fans. Not a dry eye in the house. The Dome in Brighton won't be big enough. I need the biggest stage there is. I'm the biggest star. The best fucking singer in the whole world. And the stage will be showered with flowers. A carpet of flowers.

Old Dot is restrained through this.

SCENE 7

Old Dot is in hospital. Maisie has arrived. It is tense.

MAISIE: Is there anything you need?

Pause.

Cup of tea? Paper? Some chocolate?

Pause.

Warm enough? Shall I ask them for another blanket?

Pause.

Oh, this is bloody ridiculous. If it makes you feel better, blame me.

OLD DOT: Oh, don't worry – I am.

MAISIE: And do you feel better?

Pause.

MAISIE: We'll have you back home in no time.

OLD DOT: No rush, is there? Least it's comfortable here.

Pause.

MAISIE: I'll leave you to it.

OLD DOT: No. Don't mind me. You don't have to go.

MAISIE: I don't want to be in your way.

OLD DOT: It's up to you.

Awkward pause.

MAISIE: Well I'll stay for a bit, if you like.

OLD DOT: Have there been any other visitors?

MAISIE: I'm sure he'll come.

OLD DOT: No visitors. Nobody.

Pause.

OLD DOT: Do you have family? Yes, of course you do. Children? I can't remember . . .

MAISIE: Chris and Sharon. Good times. House, decent-sized bathroom, nice car. What more could a woman want?

Old Dot is silent.

MAISIE: Used to sit in the kitchen of an evening. June and July. Ron would be out in the back garden, in his vegetable patch. Green fingers, see – lovely touch. Every now and then he'd look up – just for a second or two – and he'd catch my eye and we'd smile at each other. Then he'd carry on and I'd think: 'Yes, Maisie, this is good'.

OLD DOT: Alright.

MAISIE: He'd come in and have a swill and we'd sit down to watch *Coronation Street*.

OLD DOT: Don't . . .

MAISIE: All cosy-like.

OLD DOT: Alright! Don't go on. Married bliss, I get the fucking picture!
Sorry! I'm sorry, I didn't mean it!

MAISIE: Did you ever want any?

OLD DOT: Had to get rid of Billy's. Couldn't carry Roger's. Ironic, isn't it?

MAISIE: Oh, Dot. I'm sorry. Cruel.

OLD DOT: My gynae in Hollywood, he said to me: 'Get Roger to take these pills'. Had my legs in the air for weeks, and in the end it worked – I was up the spout. 'You'll have to lie on your back for six months', they said. 'Can't', I said, 'I have a tour to promote'. Slave to the Song, see.

MAISIE: God, He blessed you with a voice, He did. Why don't you rest for a while?

OLD DOT: Give me your hand. Come on, Maisie, give me your hand.

They hold hands.

OLD DOT: The Song – it took everything. Lost everything. My beautiful house – gone. In flames. Everything. My piano, jewellery, furniture. I ran back in, you know. Managed to save my letters. Couldn't save Jason.

MAISIE: Jason?

OLD DOT: He was always there for me. My best friend.

MAISIE: Oh my God! I don't remember reading about that.

OLD DOT: Jason. My poodle.

MAISIE: Oh!

OLD DOT: Emily found him underneath the grand piano, both burnt to a cinder. She was so kind to me that day! Stubborn, like a mule, just like her father . . . a chip off the old block she was.

MAISIE: Emily?

OLD DOT: Never mind.

MAISIE: Shall I call her . . . ?

Old Dot is silent. She closes her eyes.
Maisie leaves to make a phone call.

SCENE 8

Hospital. Old Dot is sleeping. Emily arrives. She sees Dot. She gets cold feet. She turns to leave, but comes face to face with Maisie.

MAISIE:	Yes . . . ? Can I help you? She's not seeing anybody at the moment.
EMILY:	It's alright, I'm leaving!
MAISIE:	I could make you an appointment.
EMILY:	You must be Maisie.
MAISIE:	That's right! I'm keeping an eye on things. Looking after her diary!
EMILY:	I'm Emily.
MAISIE:	Ah!
EMILY:	Niece.
MAISIE:	I do know that.
EMILY:	Of course.
MAISIE:	Funny.
EMILY:	What is . . . ?
MAISIE:	Some people – they don't look anything like their voices! Your telephone voice anyway . . .

Pause.

EMILY: How is she?

MAISIE: Comfortable.

EMILY: Is she?

MAISIE: It's cancer.

EMILY: I'd heard a rumour.

MAISIE: Took your time getting here.

Old Dot opens her eyes.

OLD DOT: Maisie?

Old Dot and Emily see one another.

MAISIE: Shall I leave you to it?

Old Dot nods.
Maisie exits.

EMILY: Auntie Dorothy . . . ?

Pause.

               How are you?

Emily moves forward to greet her.

OLD DOT: You've gone fat.

EMILY: It's good to see you too.

OLD DOT: You look older. Mind you, eight years is a long time.

EMILY: It's never been that long . . .

OLD DOT: What happened to your other half?

EMILY: Who do you mean?

OLD DOT: Dwight; Dexter . . . Whatever his name is. That married creep.

EMILY: David and I finished a long time ago.

OLD DOT: Promised to leave his wife for you, didn't he? They all do that. Not surprised he didn't, mind, the way you've let yourself go! Would've broken any man's heart. Been anyone else?

EMILY: Really?

OLD DOT: (*She notices the absence of a ring*)
Oh, no . . .

EMILY: I could be. I could've been. I've a great job. I'm busy.

OLD DOT: Snowed under, I'd say.

EMILY: I have been looking for you, Auntie Dorothy!

OLD DOT: Hmmm . . .

EMILY:	Kept in touch with all the people we knew . . .
OLD DOT:	Short memories, the lot of 'em! Fair weather friends . . .
EMILY:	It was hard. I had no idea where you were and . . .
OLD DOT:	Never far from the papers.
EMILY:	Must've been reading the wrong papers.

Pause.

> Could we stop this? Could we please . . . just stop. It's not as if you've gone away! I've had all sorts badgering me, over the years. All sorts – lawyers, accountants, journalists, Inland Revenue. I've had to deal with a lot of stuff in your absence.

OLD DOT:	My absence? You should slam the phone down. It's simple.
EMILY:	Isn't it?! Out of sight, out of mind.
OLD DOT:	I've never felt that.
EMILY:	Then why won't you give me a hug?
OLD DOT:	Because the weight of your body might burst this bag and you'd have piss all over you.

Emily laughs spontaneously.

EMILY: Don't leave the two of us in a mess. Can't we at least call it quits?

OLD DOT: You want me to forgive you?

EMILY: Let's just forgive each other. We're still blood!

OLD DOT: Blood? Not when it mattered!

EMILY: Is that why you put HER down as your next of kin? I've been trying to call you!

OLD DOT: She's been very kind to me.

EMILY: How do you know what she wants?

OLD DOT: What do you want, Emily?

EMILY: My Auntie Dorothy.

OLD DOT: What's that supposed to mean?!

EMILY: You're doing it again! Can't you hear yourself? Shutting me out. Denying me. Just like you denied Daddy.

OLD DOT: Oh yes! Always bringing your father into it! Well, he needs to know it wasn't my fault. I'll be with him soon. He needs to know you left of your own accord.

EMILY: I left because the situation was intolerable.

OLD DOT: I did my bit! I kept my promise to him!

EMILY: You certainly did your bit to drive me away!

OLD DOT: Why are you doing this? Why don't you just leave it to the Man upstairs?

EMILY: Well it's you who'll have to do the explaining, whoever's up there. I'm not interested in your excuses anymore. I came here looking for my Auntie Dorothy. Shame I didn't find her.

SCENE 9

Hospital. Maisie has brought a cassette player in and a bag of chips.

MAISIE: Don't tell matron. Been a nightmare smuggling these in. Don't get excited, mind – it's only fish 'n' chips again.

OLD DOT: Nothing wrong with cod-and-chips. What's that for?

MAISIE: Thought we could listen to some of your songs.

OLD DOT: That sounds nice.

Maisie hands over the bag and sits on the bed. They start eating.

Do you know what Oscar Wilde said when he was ill? He said two things, actually. Ordering yet another bottle of champagne, he said: 'I die as I have lived – beyond my means'.

Maisie smiles.

OLD DOT: And then, and then he said – staring at the rather ghastly wallpaper all around him: 'Either it goes – or I do.' Ha, ha!

MAISIE: Funny.

OLD DOT: Bloody genius.

Old Dot looks to the heavens.

OLD DOT: 'We're all in the gutter but some of us are looking at the stars.' I was the first British star at The Talk of the Town, you know. Eartha Kitt, she'd played there; so had Lena Horne; Sammy Davis too – all the big American names. But they were asking too much and not getting bums on seats. I tore the bollocks off 'em.
They all loved me. Learnt from me. Diana Dors, Tom Jones, Bassey. Elvis visited me every night for a week when I played the Moulin Rouge in Hollywood. Do you know how much I had in my purse when I married Roger?

Maisie shakes her head.

OLD DOT: Eight dollars. 'Listen', I said – I told Warner Brothers: 'He's just finished a big TV series and you'll have to pay him for that'. Roger, see? Fifteen hundred dollars a week – I got him fifteen hundred dollars a week. They were begging me to go back to England, to shoot *Stars In Their Eyes* but I said 'no'. I said, 'There's only one star in my eye'. I did all that, knowing – knowing – there were always plenty of beautiful girls hanging around. Not that I fell short of attention! Charles Coburn – he was big in those days – he used to say: 'Why don't you divorce Roger and marry me?' I used to say: 'Why don't you marry Blanche Sweet?' She was big, too – big name apparently. He said: 'Why should I marry any of them, when I can fuck them all?'

MAISIE: Go on. Tuck in.

OLD DOT: Promise me something, Maisie: Don't let
                them bury me in Port Talbot.

MAISIE: Stop that. You're not going anywhere just yet.

OLD DOT: I want to rest with my brother, Freddie.
                Promise me?

*Maisie nods. Maisie turns on the tatty cassette player that she's
brought in. 'Everything is Beautiful in its Own Way' plays.*

MAISIE: (*A cappella*)
                'Everything is beautiful . . . in its own way . . .

OLD DOT: Like a starry summer night . . .

OLD DOT / MAISIE: (*Sing*)
                Or a snow-covered winter's day
                And everybody's beautiful, in their own way
                Under God's heaven, the world's gonna find a
                way . . .'

*Maisie takes Old Dot's hand and helps her up. It is difficult and
painful for Old Dot. They cling to each other, slow-dancing as
they sing.*

OLD DOT: Look at us two old bastards!

*Old Dot and Maisie have a moment. They hug.
Emily enters.
They stop. Maisie switches off the cassette player.*

Pause.

MAISIE: I'll be back in a bit.

OLD DOT: You don't have to go.

MAISIE: See to your family.

Old Dot and Maisie share a look.
Maisie exits.

OLD DOT: Thought you'd be long gone.

EMILY: We've got unfinished business, Auntie Dorothy.

Pause.

Do you want me to apologise?

OLD DOT: For what?

EMILY: Anything, everything, you choose.

OLD DOT: I don't need your apologies. I want you to be honest with me.

EMILY: Haven't I always?

OLD DOT: Honest, maybe – but not necessarily right.

EMILY: There are no rights or wrongs, only opinions.

OLD DOT: Clever!

EMILY: One of yours.

OLD DOT: Is it?

Pause.

EMILY: There are reasons, big reasons why you haven't seen me, but if I start listing them they'll sound like excuses so I'm just going to say I'm sorry I haven't been here for you. I've thought about you every day . . .

OLD DOT: Stop it . . . We all make mistakes, bach. Even I've made mistakes! There – you've heard me say it. But you see . . . I was given this terrible hand – the Devil himself, he dealt it! Song . . . or family. I've had to play it all my life and I've struggled. But I could see everything! And . . . now that it's played out . . . I wonder . . . (*beat*) . . . I'll always fucking love you, Em – as if you were my own – that'll never change.

EMILY: I've missed you, Auntie Dorothy.

They hug

How are you feeling?

OLD DOT: I'm dying, Em.

EMILY: Stop it. Who's talking about dying?

OLD DOT: We are all dying. I thought you said you would always be honest with me. No point lying just 'cos you're afraid.

EMILY: I don't want to remember this. Let's remember all the lives we've lived.

Maisie enters with a card and flowers.

MAISIE: These were waiting for you in reception.

OLD DOT: What does it say on the card?

Maisie passes the card to Emily. They share a look.

MAISIE: Here.

EMILY: (*Reading*)
              'With love. From Roger.'.

OLD DOT: Magic!

Emily puts the card away. Maisie gives Old Dot the flowers. Old Dot presses the flowers to her bosom.

OLD DOT: Magic. Put them in some water for me, Em.

MAISIE: First of many, Dot. Once you get well you'll have the world at your feet! Brighton is only the beginning . . .

EMILY: Just like old times, Auntie Dorothy.

OLD DOT: No, girls. I don't think so.
              I can't sing anymore.

EMILY: It doesn't matter. It's all here.

Young Dot sings 'If I Never Sing Another Song'.

YOUNG DOT: (*Sings*)

> 'In my heyday, young men wrote to me
> Everybody seemed to have time to devote
> to me
> Everyone I saw swore they knew me
> Once upon a song
> Main attraction, couldn't buy a seat
>
> If I never sing another song
> It wouldn't bother me
> I had my share of fame
> You know my name.'

END

Sherman Cymru Publications:
Maes Terfyn **Gwyneth Glyn**
The Almond and the Seahorse **Kaite O'Reilly**
Yr Argae **Conor McPherson – cyf. Cymraeg Wil Sam Jones**
Amgen : Broken **Gary Owen**
Ceisio'i Bywyd Hi **Martin Crimp – cyf. Cymraeg Owen Martell**
Cardboard Dad **Alan Harris**
Llwyth **Dafydd James**
Cityscape **Emily Steel, Tracy Harris, Bethan Marlow, Kit Lambert**
Gadael yr Ugeinfed Ganrif **Gareth Potter**
Cinders & Plum (...and me, Will!) **Louise Osborn**
Desire Lines **Ian Rowlands**
Sgint **Bethan Marlow**
Clytemnestra **Gwyneth Lewis**

Available from:
Sherman Cymru
Senghennydd Road,
Cardiff, CF24 4YE
029 2064 6900

Range of titles also available from:
www.shermancymru.co.uk/playtext/
www.amazon.co.uk/shops/sherman_cymru